The Tale of Thorstein Shiver

Original Text, Translations, and Word Lists

Translated by
Matthew Leigh Embleton

Copyright ©2025 Matthew Leigh Embleton. All rights reserved.

The Tale of Thorstein Shiver

The Tale of Thorstein Shiver (*Old Norse*) 4
Word List *(Old Norse to English)* 12
Word List *(English to Old Norse)* 18
The Tale of Thorstein Shiver (*Old Icelandic*) 24
Word List *(Old Icelandic to English)* 32
Word List *(English to Old Icelandic)* 38
A Word Comparison of Old Norse and Old Icelandic Words 44

Cover: Old Norse text over an outline of Iceland. Author's design.

The original Old Norse and Old Icelandic texts are in the public domain.
These translations ©2022 Matthew Leigh Embleton
©2025 Matthew Leigh Embleton (This Edition)

Acknowledgments

I have long been fascinated by languages and history, and I am very grateful to the special people in my life who have supported and encouraged me in my work. Thank you for believing in me. You know who you are.

Introduction

Old Norse is a North Germanic language spoken by inhabitants of Scandinavia from about the 7th to the 15th centuries. Old Icelandic is a variety of Old West Norse that emerged during the Norse settlement of Iceland in the second half of the 9th century. The rich tradition of Icelandic literature survived by oral tradition over several centuries before being written down in the 13th Century. The Tale of Thorstein Shiver (*Þorsteins þáttr skelks*) is one of the many Tales of Icelanders or *Íslendingaþættir*. The word '*þáttr*' (plural: '*þættir*') translates as a strand of rope or a yarn, comparable to the word 'yarn' in English sometimes used to refer to a story.

This book contains:
- The Tale of Thorstein Shiver (*Þorsteins þáttr skelks*) (Old Norse Version)
- An Old Norse to English Word List
- An English to Old Norse Word List
- The Tale of Thorstein Shiver (*Þorsteins þáttr skelks*) (Old Icelandic Version)
- An Old Icelandic to English Word List
- An English to Old Icelandic Word List
- A Word Comparison of Old Norse and Old Icelandic words

The texts are presented in their original form, with a literal word-for-word line-by-line translation, and a Modern English translation, all side-by-side. In this way, it is possible to see and feel how the worked and how it has evolved. This book is designed to be of use and interest to anyone with a passion for the Old Norse or Old Icelandic language, Norse history, or languages and history in general.

The Tale of Thorstein Shiver (*Old Norse*)

Old Norse	Literal	English
1	**1**	**1**
Þat er sagt, um sumarit eftir, at Óláfr konungr fór at veizlum austr um Víkina ok víðara annars staðar..	It is said, about summer following, that Olaf the-king went to feasts east around Vik and wider other places..	It is said that the following summer, King Olaf went to feasts in the east around Vik and wider to other places.
Tók hann veizlu á þeim bæ, er á Reinu heitir..	Took he a-feast with them a-farm, which was Reim named..	He took a feast at a farm called Reim.
Hann var mjök fjölmennr..	He was-with many followers..	He was with many followers.
Sá var maðr þá með konungi, er Þorsteinn hét Þorkelsson, Ásgeirssonar æðikolls, Auðunarsonar skökuls, íslenzkr maðr, ok hafði komit til konungs um vetrinn áðr..	So was a-man there with the-king, who-was Thorstein named Son-of-Thorkel, Son-of-Asgeir rage-head, Son-of-Audun shaft, Icelandic man, and had come to the-king's about winter before..	Also there with the king was a man named Thorstein, the son of Thorkel, the son of Asgeir Rage-Head, son of Audun Shaft, an Icelander man, and he had come to the king around the winter before.
Um kveldit, er menn sátu yfir drykkjuborðum, talaði Óláfr konungr, at engi maðr af hans mönnum skyldi einn saman fara í salerni um náttina, því at hverr, sem ganga beiddist, skyldi með sér kalla sinn rekkjufélaga, ella kvað hann eigi mundu hlýða..	About evening, were the-men sitting over drinking-tables, told Olaf the-king, that no man of his men should alone together go to toilet about night-time, therefore that each, who go ask, should with them call their bed-fellow, or-else be-called him not will obey..	About evening, the men were sitting at the drinking tables, and Olaf the king made a speech, that none of his men should go alone to the toilet during the night, and that anyone who must go, should ask their bed fellow to accompany them, or they will have disobeyed him.
Drekka menn nú vel um kveldit, en er ofan váru drykkjuborð, gengu menn at sofa..	Drank the-men now well about the-evening, and when downed were drinking-tables, went men to sleep..	The men now drank well into the evening, and when the drinking tables were taken down, the men went to sleep.
Ok er á leið náttina, vaknaði Þorsteinn íslendingr ok beiddi at ganga af sæng, en sá svaf fast, er hjá honum lá, svá at Þorsteinn vildi víst eigi vekja hann..	And when that during the-night, awoke Thorstein the-Icelander and needed to go from the-bed, but so slept fast, was beside him lay, so that Thorstein willed certainly not-to awake him..	And during the night, Thorstein the Icelander awoke and needed to go from his bed, but he who was beside him was fast asleep, so that Thorstein did not want to wake him.

The Tale of Thorstein Shiver (Old Norse)

Old Norse	Literal	English
Stendr hann þá upp ok kippir skóm á fætr sér ok tekr yfir sik einn feld þykkvan ok gengr til heimilishúss..	Stood he then up and drew his-shoes about feet his and took about himself a cloak thick and went to the-outhouse..	He then stood up, put his shoes on his feet, and drew a thick cloak around him, and went to the outhouse.
Þat var stórt hús, svá at ellifu menn máttu sitja hvárum megin..	It was a-large house, so that eleven men might sit each may..	It was a large outhouse, that might have fit eleven men sitting.
Sezt hann á yztu setu,	Sat he on the-outermost seat,	He sat on the outermost seat,
ok er hann hefir setit nökkura stund, sér hann, at púki kemr upp á innstu setu ok sat þar..	and as he had sat some while, saw he, that a-demon came up from the-innermost seat and sat there..	and as he sat there for a while, he saw that a demon came up from the innermost seat and sat there.
Þorsteinn mælti þá:.	Thorstein spoke then:.	Then Thorstein spoke:
"Hverr er þar kominn?"	"Who is that come?"	"Who is that there?"
Dólgrinn svarar:.	The-demon answered:.	The-demon answered:
"Hér er kominn Þorkell inn þunni, er fell á hræ með Haraldi konungi hilditönn"..	"Here is come Thorkel the thin, who fell about corpses with Harald the-king war-tooth".	"Here is Thorkel the Thin, who fell about corpses with king Harald Wartooth".
"Hvaðan kom þú nú at?"	"From-where came you now to?"	"Where did you come from?"
kvað Þorsteinn..	said Thorstein..	said Thorstein.
Hann sagðist nú nýkominn at ór helvíti..	He said now newly-come from out-of hell..	He said that he had newly come from hell.
"Hvat kanntu þaðan at segja?"	"What can-you of-there to say?"	"What can you tell me me about it there?"
spurði Þorsteinn..	asked Thorstein..	asked Thorstein.
Hinn svarar:.	He answered:.	He answered:
"Hvers villtu spyrja?".	"What will-you ask".	"What do you want to know?"
"Hverir þola bezt píslir í helvíti?".	"Who endures best the-torment in hell".	"Who endures the torments of hell best?"
"Engi betr",	"None better",	"There is none better...",

The Tale of Thorstein Shiver (Old Norse)

Old Norse	Literal	English
kvað púki,.	said the-demon,.	said the demon,
"en Sigurðr Fáfnisbani"..	"than Sigurd Fafnisbani".	"...than Sigurd Fafnisbani".
"Hverja písl hefir hann?".	"What torment has he".	"What torment does he have?"
"Hann kyndir ofn brennanda",	"He kindles the-oven burning",	"He kindles the oven burning",
sagði draugrinn..	said the-demon..	said the demon.
"Ekki þykkir mér þat svá mikil písl",	"Not seems to-me that so much torment",	"That does not seem to me to be such a torment",
segir Þorsteinn..	said Thorstein..	said Thorstein.
"Eigi er þat þó",	"Not is that though",	"It's not that though",
kvað púki,.	said the-demon,.	said the demon,
"því at hann er sjálfr kyndarinn"..	"because that he is himself the-kindling".	"Because he himself is the kindling".
"Mikit er þat þá",	"Much is that then",	"That is very much then",
kvað Þorsteinn,.	said Thorstein,.	said Thorstein.
"eða hverr þolir þar verst píslir?"	"but who endures there the-worst torment?"	"But who endures the worst torment?"
Draugrinn svarar:.	The-demon answered:.	The demon answered:
"Starkaðr inn gamli þolir verst, því at hann æpir svá, at oss fjöndunum er þat meiri pína en flest allt annat, svá at vér megum fyrir hans ópi aldri náðir hafa"..	"Starkad the old endures the-worst, because that he cries-out so, that to-us the-torment is that more torment than most all else, so that we may for his shrieking never mercy have".	"Starkad the Old endures it worst, because he cries out so much, that to us the torment is worse than anything else, so that we may have mercy from his shrieking".
"Hvat pínu hefir hann þess",	"What torment has he this",	"What torment does he have?...",
kvað Þorsteinn,.	said Thorstein,.	said Thorstein,
"er hann þolir svá illa, svá hraustr maðr sem hann hefir sagðr verit?".	"that he endures so badly, so brave a-man as he has-been said been".	"...that he endures it so badly, such a brave man as has been said to be?"

The Tale of Thorstein Shiver (Old Norse)

Old Norse	Literal	English
"Hann hefir öklaeld"..	"He has ankle-fire".	"He has fire up to his ankles".
"Ekki þykkir mér þat svá mikit",	"Not seems to-me that so much",	"That does not seem to me to be so much...",
sagði Þorsteirn,.	said Thorstein,.	said Thorstein,
"slíkum kappa sem hann hefir verit"..	"such hero as he has been".	"...such a hero as he has been".
"Ekki er þá rétt á litit",	"Not is that right all considered",	"Then you have not considered it all correctly...",
kvað draugr,.	said the-demon,.	said the demon,
"því at iljarnar einar standa upp ór eldinum"..	"because that soles-of-the-feet only stand above from the-flames".	"...because only the soles of his feet are sticking out from the flames".
"Mikit er þat",	"Much is that",	"That is a lot then",
kvað Þorsteinn,.	said Thorstein,.	said Thorstein,
"ok æp þú eftir honum nökkut óp"..	"and shriek you after him somehow cries-out".	"And now, shriek something like how he does, once".
"Þat skal vera",	"That shall be",	"So it shall be",
kvað púki..	said the-demon..	said the demon.
Hann sló þá í sundr á sér hváftunum ok setti upp gaul mikit, en Þorsteinn brá feldarskautinu at höfði sér..	He struck then to down of his cheeks and put up a-howl great, but Thorstein drew fur-cloak about head his..	He then threw open his jaws and put up a great howl, but Thorstein drew his fur cloak about his head.
Honum varð mjök ósvipt við óp þetta ok mælti:.	He was much un-thrown with shouting this and spoke:.	He remained unmoved at this shouting and spoke:
"Æpir hann þetta ópit mest svá?".	"Cries-out he this open mostly so".	"Is that the most he cries out?"
"Fjarri ferr um þat",	"Far away about that",	"Far from it...",
kvað draugr,.	said the-demon,.	said the demon,
"því at þetta er óp várt drýsildjöflanna"..	"because that this is shouting us petty-devils".	"...because that is the shouting of us petty devils".

The Tale of Thorstein Shiver (Old Norse)

Old Norse	Literal	English
"Æp þú eftir Starkaði lítt at", kvað Þorsteinn..	"Shriek you after Starkad a-little then", asked Thorstein..	"Shriek like Starkad does a little then", asked Thorstein.
"Þat má vel",	"That may well",	"So it shall be",
kvað púki..	said the-demon..	said the demon.
Tekr hann þá at æpa í annan tíma svá öskurliga, at Þorsteini þótti firn í, hversu mikit sjá fjandi, jafnlítill, gat gaulat..	Took he then to shrieking a second time so terribly, that Thorstein thought monstrous of, how-so great such a-fiend, as-small, could bellow..	He took to sheirking a second time so terribly, that Thorstein thought it was monstrous, that such a little fiend could bellow so loudly.
Þorsteinn gerir þá sem fyrr, at hann vafði feldinum at höfði sér, ok brá honum þó svá við, at ómegin var á honum, svá at hann vissi ekki til sín..	Thorstein did then as before, that he wrapped cloak about head his, and drew he then so against, that un-mighty was so he, so that he knew not to himself..	Thorstein then did as before, and wrapped his cloak around his head, but the shrieking paralysed him, and he fainted.
Þá spurði púkinn:.	Then asked the-demon:.	Then the demon asked:
"Hví þegir þú nú?"	"Why silent are-you now?"	"Who are you so quiet now?"
Þorsteinn anzaði, er af honum leið:.	Thorstein replied, that of him this-way:.	Thorstein replied to him this way:
"Því þegi ek, at ek undrumst, hvé mikil ógnarraust at liggr í þér, eigi meiri púki en mér sýnist þú vera, eða er þetta it mesta óp Starkaðar?".	"Because silent i-am, that i wonder, how great dreadful-voice that laid in you, no more demon than to-me seems you be, or was this the most shouting Of-Starkad".	"I am silent because I wonder, how such a dreadful voice came from you, little demon that you seem to be, and was this the loudes shouting of Starkad?"
"Eigi er nærri því", segir hann,.	"Not is near as", said he,.	"Not even close", he said,
"þetta er heldr it minnsta óp hans"..	"this is rather the quietest shouting his".	"This is rather like his quietest shrieking".
"Drag þú eigi undan lengr",	"Drag you not further long",	"Delay no further",
kvað Þorsteinn,.	said Thorstein,.	said Thorstein,
"ok lát mik heyra it mesta ópit"..	"and let me hear the most shriek".	"And let me hear the loudest shriek".

The Tale of Thorstein Shiver (Old Norse)

Old Norse	Literal	English
Púki játaði því..	The-demon agreed accordingly..	The demon agreed accordingly.
Þorsteinn bjóst þá við ok braut saman feldinn ok snaraði hann svá at höfði sér ok helt at útan báðum höndum..	Thorstein prepared then with and brought together cloak and snared it so about head his and held at of both hands..	Thorstein then prepared himself by folding the cloak, winding it around his head, and holding it with both hands.
Draugrinn hafði þokat at Þorsteini um þrjár setur við hvert ópit, ok váru þá þrjár einar á milli þeira..	The-demon had moved to Thorstein about three seats with each shriek, and was then three only in between them..	The demon had moved closer to Thorstein by three seats with each shriek, and there were only three seats between them.
Púkinn belgði þá hræðiliga hváftana ok sneri um í sér augunum ok tók at gaula svá hátt, at Þorsteini þótti ór hófi keyra, ok í því kvað við klukkan í staðnum, en Þorsteinn fell í óvit fram á gólfit..	The-demon bellowed then terribly cheeks and turned about in his eyes and took to howling so high, that Thorstein thought out-of measure exceeded, and at since cried-out with the-clock about the-place, then Thorstein fell to unconscious towards the floor..	The demon then bellowed his cheeks terribly and rolled his eyes, and began howling so loudly, that it was beyond all measure for Thorstein, and as he cried out, the church bell rang out, and Thorstein fell unconscious to the floor.
En púkanum brá svá við klukkuhljóðit, at hann steypðist niðr í gólfit, ok mátti lengi heyra yminn niðr í jörðina..	Then the-demon drew so against the-clock-sound, that he fell down to the-floor, and may long be-heard the-sound down in the-earth..	The demon reacted to the bell by tumbling to the floor, the sound could be heard for a long time down in the earth.
Þorsteinn raknaði skjótt við ok stóð upp ok gekk til sængr sinnar ok lagðist niðr..	Thorstein recovered quickly with and stood up and went to bed his and lay down..	Thorstein recovered quickly, stood up, went to his bed and lay down.

2

En er morgnaði, stóðu menn upp..	When it-was morning, stood the-men up..	When it was morning, the men stood up.
Gekk konungr til kirkju ok hlýddi tíðum..	Went the-king to church and obeyed often..	The king went to the church in his religious obedience.
Eftir þat var gengit til borða..	After that then went to the-table..	Then after that they went to the table to eat.
Konungr var ekki foraðs blíðr..	The-King was not terribly happy..	The king was not terribly happy.
Hann tók til orða:.	He took to words:.	He began to speak:

The Tale of Thorstein Shiver (Old Norse)

Old Norse	Literal	English
"Hefir nökkurr maðr farit einn saman í nátt til heimilishúss?"	"Had some man travelled alone together in the-night to-the outhouse?"	"Did somebody go alone in the night to the outhouse?"
Þorsteinn stóð þá upp ok fell fram fyrir konung ok sagðist af hafa brugðit hans boði..	Thorstein stood then up and fell forwards before the-king and said out-of had custom he asked..	Thorstein then stood up and fell before the king and said that he had disobeyed his order.
Konungr svarar:.	The-King answered:.	The king answered:
"Ekki var mér þetta svá mikil meingerð, en sýnir þú þat, sem talat er til yðvar íslendinga, at þér séð mjök einrænir, en varð þú við nökkut varr?"	"Not was to-me this so great offence, but showed you that, which-is told that to your Icelanders, that they seem very-much stubborn, but were you with something aware?"	"It was not so great an offence to me, but it shows what is said about you Icelanders, that you are very stubborn, but were you aware of something?"
Þorsteinn sagði þá alla sögu, sem farit hafði..	Thorstein said then all said, as went had..	Thorstein then told him all that had happened.
Konungr spurði:.	The-King asked:.	The king asked:
"Hví þótti þér gagn, at hann æpði?".	"Why seemed to-you benefit, that he shrieked".	"What benefit did you seek from his shrieking?"
"Þat vil ek segja yðr, herra..	"That will i say to-you, lord..	"I will tell you, lord.
Ek þóttist þat vita, með því at þér höfðuð varat alla menn við at fara þangat einir saman, en skelmirinn kom upp, at vit mundim eigi klakklaust skilja, en ek ætlaða, at þér mundið vakna við, herra, er hann æpði, ok þóttumst ek þá hólpinn, ef þér yrðið varir við"..	I thought that certainly, with since that you had warned all men against to go there alone together, when the-demon came up, then knew would not unhurt know, but i supposed, that you would awake with, lord, when he shrieked, and thought i then to-be-helped, if you had-been aware with".	I thought that it was certain, that since you warned everyone against going alone, when the demon appeared, then he would not leave the place unharmed, but I supposed that if you were to wake up, lord, when he shrieked, that I might be helped, if you had been aware of it".
"Svá var ok",	"So was and",	"So it was, and...",
sagði konungr,.	said the-king,.	said the king,
"at ek vaknaða við, ok svá vissa ek, hvat fram fór, ok því lét ek hringja, at ek vissa, at eigi mundi þér ella duga..	"that i woke-up with, and so knew i, what from-going forwards, and accordingly had i rung, that i knew, that not would you otherwise be-helped..	"...at this I woke up, and I knew what was happening, and accordingly I had the church bells rung, as I knew, that nothing else could help you.

The Tale of Thorstein Shiver (Old Norse)

Old Norse	Literal	English
En hræddist þú ekki, þá er púkinn tók at æpa?"	But frightened you not, then when the-demon took to shrieking?"	But were you not frightened then, when you heard the demon shrieking?"
Þorsteinn svarar:.	Thorstein answered:.	Thorstein answered:
"Ek veit ekki, hvat þat er, hræðslan, herra"..	"I know not, how to be, afraid, lord".	"I do not know how to be afraid, lord".
"Var engi ótti í brjósti þér?"	"Was no fear in breast yours?"	"Was there no fear in your breast?",
sagði konungr..	said the-king..	said the king.
"Eigi var þat",	"None was that",	"That was not so...",
sagði Þorsteinn,.	said Thorstein,.	said Thorstein,
"því at við it síðasta ópit skaut mér næsta skelk í bringu"..	"then that with the last shriek shot me next-to shivered in chest".	"...because with that last shriek, I nearly shivered in my chest".
Konungr svarar:.	The-King answered:.	The-king answered:
"Nú skal auka nafn þitt ok kalla þik Þorstein skelk heðan af, ok er hér sverð, at ek vil gefa þér at nafnfesti"..	"Now shall extra name yours and call you Thorstein shiver from-here of, and is here a-sword, that i wish to-give to-you as a-nickname".	"Now I shall add an extra name to yours and call you Thorstein Shiver from now on, and here is a sword, that I wish to give you for your nickname".
Þorsteinn þakkaði honum..	Thorstein thanked him..	Thorstein thanked him.
Svá er sagt, at Þorsteinn gerðist hirðmaðr Óláfs konungs ok var með honum síðan ok fell á Orminum langa með öðrum köppum konungs..	So was said, that Thorstein became court-man Olaf's the-king and was with him since and fell on The-serpent long with other champions the-king's..	And so it was said, that Thorstein became a court man of King Olaf and was with him ever since, until he fell on Olaf's longship 'The Serpent' alongside the king's other champions.

Word List *(Old Norse to English)*

Old Norse	English

A, a

af	from, of, of, out-of
aldri	never
alla	all, all
allt	all
annan	second
annars	other
annat	else
anzaði	replied
at	about, as, at, from, that, then, to
auðunarsonar	son-of-Audun (name)
augunum	eyes
auka	extra
austr	east

Á, á

á	about, all, from, in, of, on, so, that, the, was, with
áðr	before
ásgeirssonar	son-of-Asgeir (name)

Æ, æ

æðikolls	rage-head
æp	shriek
æpa	shrieking
æpði	shrieked
æpir	cries-out
ætlaða	supposed

B, b

báðum	both
bæ	a-farm
beiddi	needed
beiddist	ask
belgði	bellowed
betr	better
bezt	best
bjóst	prepared
blíðr	happy
boði	asked
borða	the-table
brá	drew
braut	brought
brennanda	burning
bringu	chest
brjósti	breast
brugðit	custom

D, d

dólgrinn	the-demon
drag	drag
draugr	the-demon
draugrinn	the-demon
drekka	drank
drykkjuborð	drinking-tables
drykkjuborðum	drinking-tables
drýsildjöflanna	petty-devils
duga	be-helped

E, e

eða	but, or
ef	if
eftir	after, following
eigi	no, none, not, not-to
einar	only
einir	alone
einn	a, alone
einrænir	stubborn
ek	I, I-am
ekki	not
eldinum	the-flames
ella	or-else, otherwise
ellifu	eleven

Word List (Old Norse to English)

Old Norse	English
en	and, but, than, then, when
engi	no, none
er	as, be, is, it-was, that, was, were, when, which, who, who-was

F, f

Old Norse	English
fætr	feet
fáfnisbani	Fafnisbani (name)
fara	go
farit	travelled, went
fast	fast
feld	cloak
feldarskautinu	fur-cloak
feldinn	cloak
feldinum	cloak
fell	fell
ferr	away
firn	monstrous
fjandi	a-fiend
fjarri	far
fjölmennr	followers
fjöndunum	the-torment
flest	most
fór	forwards, went
foraðs	terribly
fram	forwards, from-going, towards
fyrir	before, for
fyrr	before

G, g

Old Norse	English
gagn	benefit
gamli	old
ganga	go
gat	could
gaul	a-howl
gaula	howling
gaulat	bellow
gefa	to-give
gekk	went
gengit	went
gengr	went
gengu	went
gerðist	became
gerir	did
gólfit	floor, the-floor

H, h

Old Norse	English
hafa	had, have
hafði	had
hann	he, him, it
hans	he, his
haraldi	Harald (name)
hátt	high
heðan	from-here
hefir	had, has, has-been
heimilishúss	outhouse, the-outhouse
heitir	named
heldr	rather
helt	held
helvíti	hell
hér	here
herra	lord
hét	named
heyra	be-heard, hear
hilditönn	war-tooth
hinn	he
hirðmaðr	court-man
hjá	beside
hlýða	obey
hlýddi	obeyed
höfði	head
höfðuð	had
hófi	measure
hólpinn	to-be-helped
höndum	hands
honum	he, him
hræ	corpses
hræddist	frightened
hræðiliga	terribly
hræðslan	afraid
hraustr	brave
hringja	rung

Word List (Old Norse to English)

Old Norse	English
hús	house
hvaðan	from-where
hváftana	cheeks
hváftunum	cheeks
hvárum	each
hvat	how, what
hvé	how
hverir	who
hverja	what
hverr	each, who
hvers	what
hversu	how-so
hvert	each
hví	why

I, i

iljarnar	soles-of-the-feet
illa	badly
inn	the
innstu	the-innermost
it	the

Í, í

í	a, about, at, in, of, to
íslendinga	Icelanders
íslendingr	the-Icelander
íslenzkr	Icelandic

J, j

jafnlítill	as-small
játaði	agreed
jörðina	the-earth

K, k

kalla	call
kanntu	can-you
kappa	hero
kemr	came

Old Norse	English
keyra	exceeded
kippir	drew
kirkju	church
klaklaust	unhurt
klukkan	the-clock
klukkuhljóðit	the-clock-sound
kom	came
kominn	come
komit	come
konung	the-king
konungi	the-king
konungr	the-king
konungs	the-king, the-king's
köppum	champions
kvað	asked, be-called, cried-out, said
kveldit	evening, the-evening
kyndarinn	the-kindling
kyndir	kindles

L, l

lá	lay
lagðist	lay
langa	long
lát	let
leið	during, this-way
lengi	long
lengr	long
lét	had
liggr	laid
litit	considered
lítt	a-little

M, m

má	may
maðr	a-man, man
mælti	spoke
mátti	may
máttu	might
með	with
megin	may
megum	may

Word List (Old Norse to English)

Old Norse	English
meingerð	offence
meiri	more
menn	men, the-men
mér	me, to-me
mest	mostly
mesta	most
mik	me
mikil	great, much
mikit	great, much
milli	between
minnsta	quietest
mjök	many, much, very-much
mönnum	men
morgnaði	morning
mundi	would
mundið	would
mundim	would
mundu	will

N, n

Old Norse	English
náðir	mercy
nærri	near
næsta	next-to
nafn	name
nafnfesti	a-nickname
nátt	the-night
náttina	night-time, the-night
niðr	down
nökkura	some
nökkurr	some
nökkut	somehow, something
nú	now
nýkominn	newly-come

O, o

Old Norse	English
ofan	downed
ofn	the-oven
ok	and
orða	words
orminum	the-serpent
oss	to-us

Ó, ó

Old Norse	English
ógnarraust	dreadful-voice
óláfr	Olaf (name)
óláfs	Olaf's (name)
ómegin	un-mighty
óp	cries-out, shouting
ópi	shrieking
ópit	open, shriek
ór	from, out-of
ósvipt	un-thrown
ótti	fear
óvit	unconscious

Ö, ö

Old Norse	English
öðrum	other
öklaeld	ankle-fire
öskurliga	terribly

P, p

Old Norse	English
pína	torment
pínu	torment
písl	torment
píslir	the-torment, torment
púkanum	the-demon
púki	a-demon, demon, the-demon
púkinn	the-demon

R, r

Old Norse	English
raknaði	recovered
reinu	Reim (place)
rekkjufélaga	bed-fellow
rétt	right

S, s

Old Norse	English
sá	so

Word List (Old Norse to English)

Old Norse	English
sæng	the-bed
sængr	bed
sagði	said
sagðist	said
sagðr	said
sagt	said
salerni	toilet
saman	together
sat	sat
sátu	sitting
séð	seem
segir	said
segja	say
sem	as, which-is, who
sér	his, saw, them
setit	sat
setti	put
setu	seat
setur	seats
sezt	sat
síðan	since
síðasta	last
sigurðr	Sigurd (name)
sik	himself
sín	himself
sinn	their
sinnar	his
sitja	sit
sjá	such
sjálfr	himself
skal	shall
skaut	shot
skelk	shiver, shivered
skelmirinn	the-demon
skilja	know
skjótt	quickly
skökuls	shaft
skóm	his-shoes
skyldi	should
slíkum	such
sló	struck
snaraði	snared
sneri	turned
sofa	sleep
sögu	said

Old Norse	English
spurði	asked
spyrja	ask
staðar	places
staðnum	the-place
standa	stand
starkaðar	of-Starkad (name)
starkaði	Starkad (name)
starkaðr	Starkad (name)
stendr	stood
steypðist	fell
stóð	stood
stóðu	stood
stórt	a-large
stund	while
sumarit	summer
sundr	down
svá	so
svaf	slept
svarar	answered
sverð	a-sword
sýnir	showed
sýnist	seems

T, t

Old Norse	English
talaði	told
talat	told
tekr	took
tíðum	often
til	to, to-the
tíma	time
tók	took

Þ, þ

Old Norse	English
þá	that, then, there
þaðan	of-there
þakkaði	thanked
þangat	there
þar	that, there
þat	it, that, to
þegi	silent
þegir	silent
þeim	them

Word List (Old Norse to English)

Old Norse	English
þeira	them
þér	they, to-you, you, yours
þess	this
þetta	this
þik	you
þitt	yours
þó	then, though
þokat	moved
þola	endures
þolir	endures
þorkell	Thorkel (name)
þorkelsson	son-of-Thorkel (name)
þorstein	Thorstein (name)
þorsteini	Thorstein (name)
þorsteinn	Thorstein (name)
þorsteirm	Thorstein (name)
þótti	seemed, thought
þóttist	thought
þóttumst	thought
þrjár	three
þú	are-you, you
þunni	thin
því	accordingly, as, because, since, then, therefore
þykkir	seems
þykkvan	thick

U, u

um	about, around
undan	further
undrumst	wonder
upp	above, up

Ú, ú

útan	of

V, v

vafði	wrapped
vakna	awake
vaknaða	woke-up
vaknaði	awoke
var	then, was, was-with
varat	warned
varð	was, were
varir	aware
varr	aware
várt	us
váru	was, were
veit	know
veizlu	a-feast
veizlum	feasts
vekja	awake
vel	well
vér	we
vera	be
verit	been
verst	the-worst
vetrinn	winter
við	against, with
víðara	wider
víkina	Vik (place)
vil	will, wish
vildi	willed
villtu	will-you
vissa	knew
vissi	knew
víst	certainly
vit	knew
vita	certainly

Y, y

yðr	to-you
yðvar	your
yfir	about, over
yminn	the-sound
yrðið	had-been
yztu	the-outermost

Word List *(English to Old Norse)*

English	Old Norse
A, a	
a	einn, í
about	á, at, í, um, yfir
above	upp
accordingly	því
a-demon	púki
a-farm	bæ
a-feast	veizlu
a-fiend	fjandi
afraid	hræðslan
after	eftir
against	við
agreed	játaði
a-howl	gaul
a-large	stórt
a-little	lítt
all	á, alla, alla, allt
alone	einir, einn
a-man	maðr
and	en, ok
a-nickname	nafnfesti
ankle-fire	öklaeld
answered	svarar
are-you	þú
around	um
as	at, er, sem, því
ask	beiddist, spyrja
asked	boði, kvað, spurði
as-small	jafnlítill
a-sword	sverð
at	at, í
awake	vakna, vekja
aware	varir, varr
away	ferr
awoke	vaknaði
B, b	
badly	illa
be	er, vera
be-called	kvað
became	gerðist
because	því
bed	sængr
bed-fellow	rekkjufélaga
been	verit
before	áðr, fyrir, fyrr
be-heard	heyra
be-helped	duga
bellow	gaulat
bellowed	belgði
benefit	gagn
beside	hjá
best	bezt
better	betr
between	milli
both	báðum
brave	hraustr
breast	brjósti
brought	braut
burning	brennanda
but	eða, en
C, c	
call	kalla
came	kemr, kom
can-you	kanntu
certainly	víst, vita
champions	köppum
cheeks	hváftana, hváftunum
chest	bringu
church	kirkju
cloak	feld, feldinn, feldinum
come	kominn, komit
considered	litit
corpses	hræ
could	gat
court-man	hirðmaðr
cried-out	kvað
cries-out	æpir, óp
custom	brugðit

Word List (English to Old Norse)

English	Old Norse	*English*	Old Norse
		from-going	fram
		from-here	heðan
D, d		*from-where*	hvaðan
		fur-cloak	feldarskautinu
demon	púki	*further*	undan
did	gerir		
down	niðr, sundr	**G, g**	
downed	ofan		
drag	drag	*go*	fara, ganga
drank	drekka	*great*	mikil, mikit
dreadful-voice	ógnarraust		
drew	brá, kippir	**H, h**	
drinking-tables	drykkjuborð, drykkjuborðum		
during	leið	*had*	hafa, hafði, hefir, höfðuð, lét
		had-been	yrðið
E, e		*hands*	höndum
		happy	blíðr
each	hvárum, hverr, hvert	*Harald (name)*	haraldi
east	austr	*has*	hefir
eleven	ellifu	*has-been*	hefir
else	annat	*have*	hafa
endures	þola, þolir	*he*	hann, hans, hinn, honum
evening	kveldit	*head*	höfði
exceeded	keyra	*hear*	heyra
extra	auka	*held*	helt
eyes	augunum	*hell*	helvíti
		here	hér
F, f		*hero*	kappa
		high	hátt
Fafnisbani (name)	fáfnisbani	*him*	hann, honum
far	fjarri	*himself*	sik, sín, sjálfr
fast	fast	*his*	hans, sér, sinnar
fear	ótti	*his-shoes*	skóm
feasts	veizlum	*house*	hús
feet	fætr	*how*	hvat, hvé
fell	fell, steypðist	*howling*	gaula
floor	gólfit	*how-so*	hversu
followers	fjölmennr		
following	eftir	**I, i**	
for	fyrir		
forwards	fór, fram	*I*	ek
frightened	hræddist		
from	á, af, at, ór		

Word List (English to Old Norse)

English	Old Norse
I-am	ek
Icelanders	íslendinga
Icelandic	íslenzkr
if	ef
in	á, í
is	er
it	hann, þat
it-was	er

K, k

kindles	kyndir
knew	vissa, vissi, vit
know	skilja, veit

L, l

laid	liggr
last	síðasta
lay	lá, lagðist
let	lát
long	langa, lengi, lengr
lord	herra

M, m

man	maðr
many	mjök
may	má, mátti, megin, megum
me	mér, mik
measure	hófi
men	menn, mönnum
mercy	náðir
might	máttu
monstrous	firn
more	meiri
morning	morgnaði
most	flest, mesta
mostly	mest
moved	þokat
much	mikil, mikit, mjök

N, n

name	nafn
named	heitir, hét
near	nærri
needed	beiddi
never	aldri
newly-come	nýkominn
next-to	næsta
night-time	náttina
no	eigi, engi
none	eigi, engi
not	eigi, ekki
not-to	eigi
now	nú

O, o

obey	hlýða
obeyed	hlýddi
of	á, af, af, í, útan
offence	meingerð
of-Starkad (name)	starkaðar
often	tíðum
of-there	þaðan
Olaf (name)	óláfr
Olaf's (name)	óláfs
old	gamli
on	á
only	einar
open	ópit
or	eða
or-else	ella
other	annars, öðrum
otherwise	ella
outhouse	heimilishúss
out-of	af, ór
over	yfir

P, p

petty-devils	drýsildjöflanna
places	staðar

Word List (English to Old Norse)

English	Old Norse
prepared	bjóst
put	setti

Q, q

quickly	skjótt
quietest	minnsta

R, r

rage-head	æðikolls
rather	heldr
recovered	raknaði
Reim (place)	reinu
replied	anzaði
right	rétt
rung	hringja

S, s

said	kvað, sagði, sagðist, sagðr, sagt, segir, sögu
sat	sat, setit, sezt
saw	sér
say	segja
seat	setu
seats	setur
second	annan
seem	séð
seemed	þótti
seems	sýnist, þykkir
shaft	skökuls
shall	skal
shiver	skelk
shivered	skelk
shot	skaut
should	skyldi
shouting	óp
showed	sýnir
shriek	æp, ópit
shrieked	æpði
shrieking	æpa, ópi

English	Old Norse
Sigurd (name)	sigurðr
silent	þegi, þegir
since	síðan, því
sit	sitja
sitting	sátu
sleep	sofa
slept	svaf
snared	snaraði
so	á, sá, svá
soles-of-the-feet	iljarnar
some	nökkura, nökkurr
somehow	nökkut
something	nökkut
son-of-Asgeir (name)	ásgeirssonar
son-of-Audun (name)	auðunarsonar
son-of-Thorkel (name)	þorkelsson
spoke	mælti
stand	standa
Starkad (name)	starkaði, starkaðr
stood	stendr, stóð, stóðu
struck	sló
stubborn	einrænir
such	sjá, slíkum
summer	sumarit
supposed	ætlaða

T, t

terribly	foraðs, hræðiliga, öskurliga
than	en
thanked	þakkaði
that	á, at, er, þá, þar, þat
the	á, inn, it
the-bed	sæng
the-clock	klukkan
the-clock-sound	klukkuhljóðit
the-demon	dólgrinn, draugr, draugrinn, púkanum, púki, púkinn, skelmirinn
the-earth	jörðina
the-evening	kveldit
the-flames	eldinum

Word List (English to Old Norse)

English	Old Norse
the-floor	gólfit
the-Icelander	íslendingr
the-innermost	innstu
their	sinn
the-kindling	kyndarinn
the-king	konung, konungi, konungr, konungs
the-king's	konungs
them	sér, þeim, þeira
the-men	menn
then	at, en, þá, þó, því, var
the-night	nátt, náttina
the-outermost	yztu
the-outhouse	heimilishúss
the-oven	ofn
the-place	staðnum
there	þá, þangat, þar
therefore	því
the-serpent	orminum
the-sound	yminn
the-table	borða
the-torment	fjöndunum, píslir
the-worst	verst
they	þér
thick	þykkvan
thin	þunni
this	þess, þetta
this-way	leið
Thorkel (name)	Þorkell
Thorstein (name)	Þorstein, Þorsteini, Þorsteinn, Þorsteirm
though	þó
thought	þótti, þóttist, þóttumst
three	þrjár
time	tíma
to	at, í, þat, til
to-be-helped	hólpinn
together	saman
to-give	gefa
toilet	salerni
told	talaði, talat
to-me	mér
took	tekr, tók
torment	pína, pínu, písl, píslir
to-the	til
to-us	oss
towards	fram
to-you	þér, yðr
travelled	farit
turned	sneri

U, u

English	Old Norse
unconscious	óvit
unhurt	klaklaust
un-mighty	ómegin
un-thrown	ósvipt
up	upp
us	várt

V, v

English	Old Norse
very-much	mjök
Vik (place)	víkina

W, w

English	Old Norse
warned	varat
war-tooth	hilditönn
was	á, er, var, varð, váru
was-with	var
we	vér
well	vel
went	farit, fór, gekk, gengit, gengr, gengu
were	er, varð, váru
what	hvat, hverja, hvers
when	en, er
which	er
which-is	sem
while	stund
who	er, hverir, hverr, sem
who-was	er
why	hví
wider	víðara
will	mundu, vil
willed	vildi
will-you	villtu
winter	vetrinn

Word List (English to Old Norse)

English	Old Norse
wish	vil
with	á, með, við
woke-up	vaknaða
wonder	undrumst
words	orða
would	mundi, mundið, mundim
wrapped	vafði

Y, y

you	þér, þik, þú
your	yðvar
yours	þér, þitt

The Tale of Thorstein Shiver (*Old Icelandic*)

Old Icelandic	Literal	English
1	**1**	**1**
Það er sagt um sumarið eftir að Ólafur konungur fór að veislum austur um Víkina og víðara annarstaðar.	It is said about summer following that Olaf the-king went to feasts east around Vik and wider other-places.	It is said that the following summer, King Olaf went to feasts in the east around Vik and wider to other places.
Tók hann veislu á þeim bæ er á Reimi heitir.	Took he a-feast with them a-farm which was Reim named.	He took a feast at a farm called Reim.
Hann var mjög fjölmennur.	He was-with many followers.	He was with many followers.
Sá var maður þá með konungi er Þorsteinn hét Þorkelsson, Ásgeirssonar æðikolls, Auðunarsonar skökuls, íslenskur maður, og hafði komið til konungs um veturinn áður.	So was a-man there with the-king who-was Thorstein named Son-of-Thorkel, Son-of-Asgeir rage-head, Son-of-Audun shaft, Icelandic man, and had come to the-king's about winter before.	Also there with the king was a man named Thorstein, the son of Thorkel, the son of Asgeir Rage-Head, son of Audun Shaft, an Icelander man, and he had come to the king around the winter before.
Um kveldið er menn sátu yfir drykkjuborðum talaði Ólafur konungur að engi maður af hans mönnum skyldi einn saman fara í salerni um náttina því að hver sem ganga beiddist skyldi með sér kalla sinn rekkjufélaga ella kvað hann eigi mundu hlýða.	About evening were the-men sitting over drinking-tables told Olaf the-king that no man of his men should alone together go to toilet about night-time therefore that each who go ask should with them call their bed-fellow or-else be-called him not will obey.	About evening, the men were sitting at the drinking tables, and Olaf the king made a speech, that none of his men should go alone to the toilet during the night, and that anyone who must go, should ask their bed fellow to accompany them, or they will have disobeyed him.
Drekka menn nú vel um kveldið en er ofan voru drykkjuborð gengu menn að sofa.	Drank the-men now well about the-evening and when downed were drinking-tables went men to sleep.	The men now drank well into the evening, and when the drinking tables were taken down, the men went to sleep.
Og er á leið náttina vaknaði Þorsteinn Íslendingur og beiddi að ganga af sæng en sá svaf fast er hjá honum lá svo að Þorsteinn vildi víst eigi vekja hann.	And when that during the-night awoke Thorstein The-Icelander and needed to go from the-bed but so slept fast was beside him lay so that Thorstein willed certainly not-to awake him.	And during the night, Thorstein the Icelander awoke and needed to go from his bed, but he who was beside him was fast asleep, so that Thorstein did not want to wake him.

The Tale of Thorstein Shiver (Old Icelandic)

Old Icelandic	Literal	English
Stendur hann þá upp og kippir skóm á fætur sér og tekur yfir sig einn feld þykkvan og gengur til heimilishúss.	Stood he then up and drew his-shoes about feet his and took about himself a cloak thick and went to the-outhouse.	He then stood up, put his shoes on his feet, and drew a thick cloak around him, and went to the outhouse.
Það var stórt hús svo að ellefu menn máttu sitja hvoru megin.	It was a-large house so that eleven men might sit each may.	It was a large outhouse, that might have fit eleven men sitting.
Sest hann á ystu setu.	Sat he on the-outermost seat.	He sat on the outermost seat,
Og er hann hefir setið nokkura stund sér hann að púki kemur upp á innstu setu og sat þar.	And as he had sat some while saw he that a-demon came up from the-innermost seat and sat there.	and as he sat there for a while, he saw that a demon came up from the innermost seat and sat there.
Þorsteinn mælti þá:	Thorstein spoke then:	Then Thorstein spoke:
"Hver er þar kominn?"	"Who is that come?"	"Who is that there?"
Dólgurinn svarar:	The-demon answered:	The-demon answered:
"Hér er kominn Þorkell hinn þunni er féll á hræ með Haraldi konungi hilditönn".	"Here is come Thorkel the thin who fell about corpses with Harald the-king war-tooth".	"Here is Thorkel the Thin, who fell about corpses with king Harald Wartooth".
"Hvaðan komst þú nú að?"	"From-where came you now to?"	"Where did you come from?"
kvað Þorsteinn.	said Thorstein.	said Thorstein.
Hann sagðist nú nýkominn að úr helvíti.	He said now newly-come from out-of hell.	He said that he had newly come from hell.
"Hvað kanntu þaðan að segja?"	"What can-you of-there to say?"	"What can you tell me me about it there?"
spurði Þorsteinn.	asked Thorstein.	asked Thorstein.
Hinn svarar:	He answered:	He answered:
"Hvers viltu spyrja?"	"What will-you ask?"	"What do you want to know?"
"Hverjir þola best píslir í helvíti?"	"Who endures best the-torment in hell?"	"Who endures the torments of hell best?"
"Engi betur",	"None better".	"There is none better...",

The Tale of Thorstein Shiver (Old Icelandic)

Old Icelandic	Literal	English
kvað púki,	said the-demon,	said the demon,
"en Sigurður Fáfnisbani".	"than Sigurd Fafnisbani".	"...than Sigurd Fafnisbani".
"Hverja písl hefir hann?"	"What torment has he?"	"What torment does he have?"
"Hann kyndir ofn brennanda",	"He kindles the-oven burning".	"He kindles the oven burning",
sagði draugurinn.	said the-demon.	said the demon.
"Ekki þykir mér það svo mikil písl",	"Not seems to-me that so much torment".	"That does not seem to me to be such a torment",
segir Þorsteinn.	said Thorstein.	said Thorstein.
"Eigi er það þó",	"Not is that though".	"It's not that though",
kvað púki,	said the-demon,	said the demon,
"því að hann er sjálfur kyndarinn".	"because that he is himself the-kindling".	"Because he himself is the kindling".
"Mikið er það þá",	"Much is that then".	"That is very much then",
kvað Þorsteinn,	said Thorstein,	said Thorstein.
"eða hver þolir þar verst píslir?"	"but who endures there the-worst torment?"	"But who endures the worst torment?"
Draugurinn svarar:	The-demon answered:	The demon answered:
"Starkaður hinn gamli þolir verst því að hann æpir svo að oss fjandunum er það meiri pína en flest allt annað svo að vér megum fyrir hans ópi aldrei náðir hafa".	"Starkad the old endures the-worst, because that he cries-out so, that to-us the-torment is that more torment than most all else, so that we may for his shrieking never mercy have".	"Starkad the Old endures it worst, because he cries out so much, that to us the torment is worse than anything else, so that we may have mercy from his shrieking".
"Hvað pínu hefir hann þess",	"What torment has he this".	"What torment does he have?...",
kvað Þorsteinn,	said Thorstein,	said Thorstein,
"er hann þolir svo illa, svo hraustur maður sem hann hefir sagður verið?"	"that he endures so badly, so brave a-man as he has-been said been?"	"...that he endures it so badly, such a brave man as has been said to be?"

The Tale of Thorstein Shiver (Old Icelandic)

Old Icelandic	Literal	English
"Hann hefir ökklaeld".	"He has ankle-fire".	"He has fire up to his ankles".
"Ekki þykir mér það svo mikið",	"Not seems to-me that so much".	"That does not seem to me to be so much...",
sagði Þorsteinn,	said Thorstein,	said Thorstein,
"slíkum kappa sem hann hefir verið".	"such hero as he has been".	"...such a hero as he has been".
"Ekki er þá rétt á litið",	"Not is that right all considered".	"Then you have not considered it all correctly...",
kvað draugur,	said the-demon,	said the demon,
"því að iljarnar einar standa upp úr eldinum".	"because that soles-of-the-feet only stand above from the-flames".	"...because only the soles of his feet are sticking out from the flames".
"Mikið er það",	"Much is that".	"That is a lot then",
kvað Þorsteinn,	said Thorstein,	said Thorstein,
"og æp þú eftir honum nokkuð óp".	"and shriek you after him somehow cries-out".	"And now, shriek something like how he does, once".
"Það skal vera",	"That shall be".	"So it shall be",
kvað púki.	said the-demon.	said the demon.
Hann sló þá í sundur á sér hvoftunum og setti upp gaul mikið en Þorsteinn brá feldarskautinu að höfði sér.	He struck then to down of his cheeks and put up a-howl great but Thorstein drew fur-cloak about head his.	He then threw open his jaws and put up a great howl, but Thorstein drew his fur cloak about his head.
Honum varð mjög ósvipt við óp þetta og mælti:	He was much un-thrown with shouting this and spoke:	He remained unmoved at this shouting and spoke:
"Æpir hann þetta ópið mest svo?"	"Cries-out he this open mostly so?"	"Is that the most he cries out?"
"Fjarri fer um það",	"Far away about that".	"Far from it...",
kvað draugur,	said the-demon,	said the demon,
"því að þetta er óp vort drýsildjöflanna".	"because that this is shouting us petty-devils".	"...because that is the shouting of us petty devils".

The Tale of Thorstein Shiver (Old Icelandic)

Old Icelandic	Literal	English
"Æp þú eftir Starkaði líttað", kvað Þorsteinn.	"Shriek you after Starkad a-little". asked Thorstein.	"Shriek like Starkad does a little then", asked Thorstein.
"Það má vel",	"That may well".	"So it shall be",
kvað púki.	said the-demon.	said the demon.
Tekur hann þá að æpa í annan tíma svo öskurlega að Þorsteini þótti firn í hversu mikið sjá fjandi jafnlítill gat gaulað.	Took he then to shrieking a second time so terribly that Thorstein thought monstrous of how-so great such a-fiend as-small could bellow.	He took to sheirking a second time so terribly, that Thorstein thought it was monstrous, that such a little fiend could bellow so loudly.
Þorsteinn gerir þá sem fyrr að hann vafði feldinum að höfði sér og brá honum þó svo við að ómegin var á honum svo að hann vissi ekki til sín.	Thorstein did then as before that he wrapped cloak about head his and drew he then so against that un-mighty was so he so that he knew not to himself.	Thorstein then did as before, and wrapped his cloak around his head, but the shrieking paralysed him, and he fainted.
Þá spurði púkinn:	Then asked the-demon:	Then the demon asked:
"Hví þegir þú nú?"	"Why silent are-you now?"	"Who are you so quiet now?"
Þorsteinn ansaði er af honum leið:	Thorstein replied that of him this-way:	Thorstein replied to him this way:
"Því þegi eg að eg undrast hve mikil ógnarraust að liggur í þér, eigi meiri púki en mér sýnist þú vera eða er þetta hið mesta óp Starkaðar?"	"Because silent i-am that i wonder how great dreadful-voice that laid in you, no more demon than to-me seems you be or was this the most shouting Of-Starkad?"	"I am silent because I wonder, how such a dreadful voice came from you, little demon that you seem to be, and was this the loudes shouting of Starkad?"
"Eigi er nærri því.	"Not is near as.	"Not even close.
Þetta er",	This is",	This is",
segir hann, "heldur hið minnsta óp hans".	said he, "rather the quietest shouting his".	he said, "rather like his quietest shrieking".
"Drag þú eigi undan lengur",	"Drag you not further long".	"Delay no further",
kvað Þorsteinn,	said Thorstein,	said Thorstein,
"og lát mig heyra hið mesta ópið".	"and let me hear the most shriek".	"And let me hear the loudest shriek".

The Tale of Thorstein Shiver (Old Icelandic)

Old Icelandic	Literal	English
Púki játtaði því.	The-demon agreed accordingly.	The demon agreed accordingly.
Þorsteinn bjóst þá við og braut saman feldinn og snaraði hann svo að höfði sér og hélt að utan báðum höndum.	Thorstein prepared then with and brought together cloak and snared it so about head his and held at of both hands.	Thorstein then prepared himself by folding the cloak, winding it around his head, and holding it with both hands.
Draugurinn hafði þokað að Þorsteini um þrjár setur við hvert ópið og voru þá þrjár einar á milli þeirra.	The-demon had moved to Thorstein about three seats with each shriek and was then three only in between them.	The demon had moved closer to Thorstein by three seats with each shriek, and there were only three seats between them.
Púkinn belgdi þá hræðilega hvoftana og sneri um í sér augunum og tók að gaula svo hátt að Þorsteini þótti úr hófi keyra og í því kvað við klukkan í staðnum en Þorsteinn féll í óvit fram á gólfið.	The-demon bellowed then terribly cheeks and turned about in his eyes and took to howling so high that Thorstein thought out-of measure exceeded and at since cried-out with the-clock about the-place then Thorstein fell to unconscious towards the floor.	The demon then bellowed his cheeks terribly and rolled his eyes, and began howling so loudly, that it was beyond all measure for Thorstein, and as he cried out, the church bell rang out, and Thorstein fell onconscious to the floor.
En púkanum brá svo við klukkuhljóðið að hann steyptist niður í gólfið og mátti lengi heyra yminn niður í jörðina.	Then the-demon drew so against the-clock-sound that he fell down to the-floor and may long be-heard the-sound down in the-earth.	The demon reacted to the bell by tumbling to the floor, the sound could be heard for a long time down in the earth.
Þorsteinn raknaði skjótt við og stóð upp og gekk til sængur sinnar og lagðist niður.	Thorstein recovered quickly with and stood up and went to bed his and lay down.	Thorstein recovered quickly, stood up, went to his bed and lay down.

2

Old Icelandic	Literal	English
En er morgnaði stóðu menn upp.	When it-was morning stood the-men up.	When it was morning, the men stood up.
Gekk konungur til kirkju og hlýddi tíðum.	Went the-king to church and obeyed often.	The king went to the church in his religious obedience.
Eftir það var gengið til borða.	After that then went to the-table.	Then after that they went to the table to eat.
Konungur var ekki forað blíður.	The-King was not terribly happy.	The king was not terribly happy.
Hann tók til orða:	He took to words:	He began to speak:

The Tale of Thorstein Shiver (Old Icelandic)

Old Icelandic	Literal	English
"Hefir nokkur maður farið einn saman í nátt til heimilishúss?"	"Had some man travelled alone together in the-night to-the outhouse?"	"Did somebody go alone in the night to the outhouse?"
Þorsteinn stóð þá upp og féll fram fyrir konung og sagðist af hafa brugðið hans boði.	Thorstein stood then up and fell forwards before the-king and said out-of had custom he asked.	Thorstein then stood up and fell before the king and said that he had disobeyed his order.
Konungur svarar:	The-King answered:	The king answered:
"Ekki var mér þetta svo mikil meingerð, en sýnir þú það sem talað er til yðvar Íslendinga að þér séuð mjög einrænir en varðst þú við nokkuð var?"	"Not was to-me this so great offence, but showed you that which-is told that to your Icelanders that they seem very-much stubborn but were you with something aware?"	"It was not so great an offence to me, but it shows what is said about you Icelanders, that you are very stubborn, but were you aware of something?"
Þorsteinn sagði þá alla sögu sem farið hafði.	Thorstein said then all said as went had.	Thorstein then told him all that had happened.
Konungur spurði:	The-King asked:	The king asked:
"Hví þótti þér gagn að hann æpti?"	"Why seemed to-you benefit that he shrieked?"	"What benefit did you seek from his shrieking?"
"Það vil eg segja yðar herra.	"That will i say to-you lord.	"I will tell you, lord.
Eg þóttist það vita með því að þér höfðuð varað alla menn við að fara þangað einir saman, en skelmirinn kom upp, að við mundum eigi klakklaust skilja en eg ætlaði að þér munduð vakna við herra er hann æpti og þóttist eg þá hólpinn ef þér yrðuð varir við".	I thought that certainly with since that you had warned all men against to go there alone together, when the-demon came up, then knew would not unhurt know but i supposed that you would awake with lord when he shrieked and thought i then to-be-helped if you had-been aware with".	I thought that it was certain, that since you warned everyone against going alone, when the demon appeared, then he would not leave the place unharmed, but I supposed that if you were to wake up, lord, when he shrieked, that I might be helped, if you had been aware of it".
"Svo var og",	"So was and".	"So it was, and...",
sagði konungur,	said the-king,	said the king,
"að eg vaknaði við og svo vissi eg hvað fram fór og því lét eg hringja að eg vissi að eigi mundi þér ella duga.	"that i woke-up with and so knew i what from-going forwards and accordingly had i rung that i knew that not would you otherwise be-helped.	"...at this I woke up, and I knew what was happening, and accordingly I had the church bells rung, as I knew, that nothing else could help you.

The Tale of Thorstein Shiver (Old Icelandic)

Old Icelandic	Literal	English
En hræddist þú ekki þá er púkinn tók að æpa?"	But frightened you not then when the-demon took to shrieking?"	But were you not frightened then, when you heard the demon shrieking?"
Þorsteinn svarar:	Thorstein answered:	Thorstein answered:
"Eg veit ekki hvað það er, hræðslan, herra".	"I know not how to be, afraid, lord".	"I do not know how to be afraid, lord".
"Var engi ótti í brjósti þér?"	"Was no fear in breast yours?"	"Was there no fear in your breast?",
sagði konungur.	said the-king.	said the king.
"Eigi var það",	"None was that".	"That was not so...",
sagði Þorsteinn,	said Thorstein,	said Thorstein,
"því að við hið síðasta ópið skaut mér næsta skelk í bringu".	"then that with the last shriek shot me next-to shivered in chest".	"...because with that last shriek, I nearly shivered in my chest".
Konungur svarar:	The-King answered:	The-king answered:
"Nú skal auka nafn þitt og kalla þig Þorstein skelk héðan af og er hér sverð að eg vil gefa þér að nafnfesti".	"Now shall extra name yours and call you Thorstein shiver from-here of and is here a-sword that i wish to-give to-you as a-nickname".	"Now I shall add an extra name to yours and call you Thorstein Shiver from now on, and here is a sword, that I wish to give you for your nickname".
Þorsteinn þakkaði honum.	Thorstein thanked him.	Thorstein thanked him.
Svo er sagt að Þorsteinn gerðist hirðmaður Ólafs konungs og var með honum síðan og féll á Orminum langa með öðrum köppum konungs.	So was said that Thorstein became court-man Olaf's the-king and was with him since and fell on The-serpent long with other champions the-king's.	And so it was said, that Thorstein became a court man of King Olaf and was with him ever since, until he fell on Olaf's longship 'The Serpent' alongside the king's other champions.

Word List *(Old Icelandic to English)*

Old Icelandic	English
A, a	
að	about, as, at, from, that, then, to
af	from, of, of, out-of
aldrei	never
alla	all, all
allt	all
annað	else
annan	second
annarstaðar	other-places
ansaði	replied
Auðunarsonar	son-of-Audun (name)
augunum	eyes
auka	extra
austur	east
Á, á	
á	about, all, from, in, of, on, so, that, the, was, with
áður	before
Ásgeirssonar	son-of-Asgeir (name)
Æ, æ	
æðikolls	rage-head
æp	shriek
æpa	shrieking
æpir	cries-out
æpti	shrieked
ætlaði	supposed
B, b	
báðum	both
bæ	a-farm
beiddi	needed
beiddist	ask
belgdi	bellowed
best	best
betur	better
bjóst	prepared
blíður	happy
boði	asked
borða	the-table
brá	drew
braut	brought
brennanda	burning
bringu	chest
brjósti	breast
brugðið	custom
D, d	
Dólgurinn	the-demon
Drag	drag
draugur	the-demon
draugurinn	the-demon
Drekka	drank
drykkjuborð	drinking-tables
drykkjuborðum	drinking-tables
drýsildjöflanna	petty-devils
duga	be-helped
E, e	
eða	but, or
ef	if
eftir	after, following
eg	I, I-am
eigi	no, none, not, not-to
einar	only
einir	alone
einn	a, alone
einrænir	stubborn
Ekki	not
eldinum	the-flames
ella	or-else, otherwise
ellefu	eleven

Word List (Old Icelandic to English)

Old Icelandic	English
en	and, but, than, then, when
engi	no, none
er	as, be, is, it-was, that, was, were, when, which, who, who-was

F, f

fætur	feet
Fáfnisbani	Fafnisbani (name)
fara	go
farið	travelled, went
fast	fast
feld	cloak
feldarskautinu	fur-cloak
feldinn	cloak
feldinum	cloak
féll	fell
fer	away
firn	monstrous
fjandi	a-fiend
fjandunum	the-torment
Fjarri	far
fjölmennur	followers
flest	most
fór	forwards, went
forað	terribly
fram	forwards, from-going, towards
fyrir	before, for
fyrr	before

G, g

gagn	benefit
gamli	old
ganga	go
gat	could
gaul	a-howl
gaula	howling
gaulað	bellow
gefa	to-give
gekk	went

Old Icelandic	English
gengið	went
gengu	went
gengur	went
gerðist	became
gerir	did
gólfið	floor, the-floor

H, h

hafa	had, have
hafði	had
hann	he, him, it
hans	he, his
Haraldi	Harald (name)
hátt	high
héðan	from-here
hefir	had, has, has-been
heimilishúss	outhouse, the-outhouse
heitir	named
heldur	rather
hélt	held
helvíti	hell
Hér	here
herra	lord
hét	named
heyra	be-heard, hear
hið	the
hilditönn	war-tooth
Hinn	he, the
hirðmaður	court-man
hjá	beside
hlýða	obey
hlýddi	obeyed
höfði	head
höfðuð	had
hófi	measure
hólpinn	to-be-helped
höndum	hands
Honum	he, him
hræ	corpses
hræddist	frightened
hræðilega	terribly
hræðslan	afraid
hraustur	brave

Word List (Old Icelandic to English)

Old Icelandic	English	*Old Icelandic*	English
hringja	rung	*kippir*	drew
hús	house	*kirkju*	church
hvað	how, what	*klakklaust*	unhurt
Hvaðan	from-where	*klukkan*	the-clock
hve	how	*klukkuhljóðið*	the-clock-sound
hver	each, who	*kom*	came
Hverja	what	*komið*	come
Hverjir	who	*kominn*	come
Hvers	what	*komst*	came
hversu	how-so	*konung*	the-king
hvert	each	*konungi*	the-king
Hví	why	*konungs*	the-king, the-king's
hvoftana	cheeks	*konungur*	the-king
hvoftunum	cheeks	*köppum*	champions
hvoru	each	*kvað*	asked, be-called, cried-out, said
		kveldið	evening, the-evening
		kyndarinn	the-kindling
		kyndir	kindles

I, i

iljarnar	soles-of-the-feet
illa	badly
innstu	the-innermost

Í, í

í	a, about, at, in, of, to
Íslendinga	Icelanders
Íslendingur	the-Icelander
íslenskur	Icelandic

J, j

jafnlítill	as-small
játtaði	agreed
jörðina	the-earth

K, k

kalla	call
kanntu	can-you
kappa	hero
kemur	came
keyra	exceeded

L, l

lá	lay
lagðist	lay
langa	long
lát	let
leið	during, this-way
lengi	long
lengur	long
lét	had
liggur	laid
litið	considered
líttað	a-little

M, m

má	may
maður	a-man, man
mælti	spoke
mátti	may
máttu	might
með	with
megin	may
megum	may

Word List (Old Icelandic to English)

Old Icelandic	English
meingerð	offence
meiri	more
menn	men, the-men
mér	me, to-me
mest	mostly
mesta	most
mig	me
mikið	great, much
mikil	great, much
milli	between
minnsta	quietest
mjög	many, much, very-much
mönnum	men
morgnaði	morning
mundi	would
mundu	will
munduð	would
mundum	would

N, n

Old Icelandic	English
náðir	mercy
nærri	near
næsta	next-to
nafn	name
nafnfesti	a-nickname
nátt	the-night
náttina	night-time, the-night
niður	down
nokkuð	somehow, something
nokkur	some
nokkura	some
nú	now
nýkominn	newly-come

O, o

Old Icelandic	English
ofan	downed
ofn	the-oven
og	and
orða	words
Orminum	the-serpent
oss	to-us

Ó, ó

Old Icelandic	English
ógnarraust	dreadful-voice
Ólafs	Olaf's (name)
Ólafur	Olaf (name)
ómegin	un-mighty
óp	cries-out, shouting
ópi	shrieking
ópið	open, shriek
ósvipt	un-thrown
ótti	fear
óvit	unconscious

Ö, ö

Old Icelandic	English
öðrum	other
ökklaeld	ankle-fire
öskurlega	terribly

P, p

Old Icelandic	English
pína	torment
pínu	torment
písl	torment
píslir	the-torment, torment
púkanum	the-demon
púki	a-demon, demon, the-demon
púkinn	the-demon

R, r

Old Icelandic	English
raknaði	recovered
Reimi	Reim (place)
rekkjufélaga	bed-fellow
rétt	right

S, s

Old Icelandic	English
Sá	so
sæng	the-bed

Word List (Old Icelandic to English)

Old Icelandic	English	Old Icelandic	English
sængur	bed	spyrja	ask
sagði	said	staðnum	the-place
sagðist	said, said	standa	stand
sagður	said	Starkaðar	of-Starkad (name)
sagt	said	Starkaði	Starkad (name)
salerni	toilet	Starkaður	Starkad (name)
saman	together	Stendur	stood
sat	sat	steyptist	fell
sátu	sitting	stóð	stood
segir	said	stóðu	stood
segja	say	stórt	a-large
sem	as, which-is, who	stund	while
sér	his, saw, them	sumarið	summer
Sest	sat	sundur	down
setið	sat	svaf	slept
setti	put	svarar	answered
setu	seat	sverð	a-sword
setur	seats	svo	so
séuð	seem	sýnir	showed
síðan	since	sýnist	seems
síðasta	last		
sig	himself		
Sigurður	Sigurd (name)		

T, t

Old Icelandic	English
sín	himself
sinn	their
sinnar	his
sitja	sit
sjá	such
sjálfur	himself
skal	shall
skaut	shot
skelk	shiver, shivered
skelmirinn	the-demon
skilja	know
skjótt	quickly
skökuls	shaft
skóm	his-shoes
skyldi	should
slíkum	such
sló	struck
snaraði	snared
sneri	turned
sofa	sleep
sögu	said
spurði	asked

talað	told
talaði	told
tekur	took
tíðum	often
til	to, to-the
tíma	time
Tók	took

Þ, þ

þá	that, then, there
Það	it, that, to
þaðan	of-there
þakkaði	thanked
þangað	there
þar	that, there
þegi	silent
þegir	silent
þeim	them
þeirra	them

Word List (Old Icelandic to English)

Old Icelandic	English
þér	they, to-you, you, yours
þess	this
þetta	this
þig	you
þitt	yours
þó	then, though
þokað	moved
þola	endures
þolir	endures
Þorkell	Thorkel (name)
Þorkelsson	son-of-Thorkel (name)
Þorstein	Thorstein (name)
Þorsteini	Thorstein (name)
Þorsteinn	Thorstein (name)
þótti	seemed, thought
þóttist	thought
þrjár	three
þú	are-you, you
þunni	thin
því	accordingly, as, because, since, then, therefore
þykir	seems
þykkvan	thick

U, u

um	about, around
undan	further
undrast	wonder
upp	above, up
utan	of

Ú, ú

úr	from, out-of

V, v

vafði	wrapped
vakna	awake
vaknaði	awoke, woke-up

Old Icelandic	English
var	aware, then, was, was-with
varað	warned
varð	was
varðst	were
varir	aware
veislu	a-feast
veislum	feasts
veit	know
vekja	awake
vel	well
vér	we
vera	be
verið	been
verst	the-worst
veturinn	winter
við	against, knew, with
víðara	wider
Víkina	Vik (place)
vil	will, wish
vildi	willed
viltu	will-you
vissi	knew
víst	certainly
vita	certainly
vort	us
voru	was, were

Y, y

yður	to-you
yðvar	your
yfir	about, over
yminn	the-sound
yrðuð	had-been
ystu	the-outermost

Word List *(English to Old Icelandic)*

English	Old Icelandic
A, a	
a	einn, í
about	á, að, í, um, yfir
above	upp
accordingly	því
a-demon	púki
a-farm	bæ
a-feast	veislu
a-fiend	fjandi
afraid	hræðslan
after	eftir
against	við
agreed	játtaði
a-howl	gaul
a-large	stórt
a-little	líttað
all	á, alla, alla, allt
alone	einir, einn
a-man	maður
and	en, og
a-nickname	nafnfesti
ankle-fire	ökklaeld
answered	svarar
are-you	þú
around	um
as	að, er, sem, því
ask	beiddist, spyrja
asked	boði, kvað, spurði
as-small	jafnlítill
a-sword	sverð
at	að, í
awake	vakna, vekja
aware	var, varir
away	fer
awoke	vaknaði
B, b	
badly	illa
be	er, vera
be-called	kvað
became	gerðist
because	því
bed	sængur
bed-fellow	rekkjufélaga
been	verið
before	áður, fyrir, fyrr
be-heard	heyra
be-helped	duga
bellow	gaulað
bellowed	belgdi
benefit	gagn
beside	hjá
best	best
better	betur
between	milli
both	báðum
brave	hraustur
breast	brjósti
brought	braut
burning	brennanda
but	eða, en
C, c	
call	kalla
came	kemur, kom, komst
can-you	kanntu
certainly	víst, vita
champions	köppum
cheeks	hvoftana, hvoftunum
chest	bringu
church	kirkju
cloak	feld, feldinn, feldinum
come	komið, kominn
considered	litið
corpses	hræ
could	gat
court-man	hirðmaður
cried-out	kvað
cries-out	æpir, óp
custom	brugðið

Word List (English to Old Icelandic)

English	Old Icelandic

D, d

demon	púki
did	gerir
down	niður, sundur
downed	ofan
drag	Drag
drank	Drekka
dreadful-voice	ógnarraust
drew	brá, kippir
drinking-tables	drykkjuborð, drykkjuborðum
during	leið

E, e

each	hver, hvert, hvoru
east	austur
eleven	ellefu
else	annað
endures	þola, þolir
evening	kveldið
exceeded	keyra
extra	auka
eyes	augunum

F, f

Fafnisbani (name)	Fáfnisbani
far	Fjarri
fast	fast
fear	ótti
feasts	veislum
feet	fætur
fell	féll, steyptist
floor	gólfið
followers	fjölmennur
following	eftir
for	fyrir
forwards	fór, fram
frightened	hræddist
from	á, að, af, úr
from-going	fram
from-here	héðan
from-where	Hvaðan
fur-cloak	feldarskautinu
further	undan

G, g

go	fara, ganga
great	mikið, mikil

H, h

had	hafa, hafði, hefir, höfðuð, lét
had-been	yrðuð
hands	höndum
happy	blíður
Harald (name)	Haraldi
has	hefir
has-been	hefir
have	hafa
he	hann, hans, Hinn, Honum
head	höfði
hear	heyra
held	hélt
hell	helvíti
here	Hér
hero	kappa
high	hátt
him	hann, honum
himself	sig, sín, sjálfur
his	hans, sér, sinnar
his-shoes	skóm
house	hús
how	hvað, hve
howling	gaula
how-so	hversu

I, i

I	eg

Word List (English to Old Icelandic)

English	Old Icelandic
I-am	eg
Icelanders	Íslendinga
Icelandic	íslenskur
if	ef
in	á, í
is	er
it	hann, Það
it-was	er

K, k

English	Old Icelandic
kindles	kyndir
knew	við, vissi
know	skilja, veit

L, l

English	Old Icelandic
laid	liggur
last	síðasta
lay	lá, lagðist
let	lát
long	langa, lengi, lengur
lord	herra

M, m

English	Old Icelandic
man	maður
many	mjög
may	má, mátti, megin, megum
me	mér, mig
measure	hófi
men	menn, mönnum
mercy	náðir
might	máttu
monstrous	firn
more	meiri
morning	morgnaði
most	flest, mesta
mostly	mest
moved	þokað
much	Mikið, mikil, mjög

N, n

English	Old Icelandic
name	nafn
named	heitir, hét
near	nærri
needed	beiddi
never	aldrei
newly-come	nýkominn
next-to	næsta
night-time	náttina
no	eigi, engi
none	Eigi, Engi
not	eigi, Ekki
not-to	eigi
now	nú

O, o

English	Old Icelandic
obey	hlýða
obeyed	hlýddi
of	á, af, af, í, utan
offence	meingerð
of-Starkad (name)	Starkaðar
often	tíðum
of-there	þaðan
Olaf (name)	Ólafur
Olaf's (name)	Ólafs
old	gamli
on	á
only	einar
open	ópið
or	eða
or-else	ella
other	öðrum
other-places	annarstaðar
otherwise	ella
outhouse	heimilishúss
out-of	af, úr
over	yfir

P, p

English	Old Icelandic
petty-devils	drýsildjöflanna

Word List (English to Old Icelandic)

English	Old Icelandic
prepared	bjóst
put	setti

Q, q

quickly	skjótt
quietest	minnsta

R, r

rage-head	æðikolls
rather	heldur
recovered	raknaði
Reim (place)	Reimi
replied	ansaði
right	rétt
rung	hringja

S, s

said	kvað, sagði, sagðist, sagðist, sagður, sagt, segir, sögu
sat	sat, Sest, setið
saw	sér
say	segja
seat	setu
seats	setur
second	annan
seem	séuð
seemed	þótti
seems	sýnist, þykir
shaft	skökuls
shall	skal
shiver	skelk
shivered	skelk
shot	skaut
should	skyldi
shouting	óp
showed	sýnir
shriek	æp, ópið
shrieked	æpti
shrieking	æpa, ópi

English	Old Icelandic
Sigurd (name)	Sigurður
silent	þegi, þegir
since	síðan, því
sit	sitja
sitting	sátu
sleep	sofa
slept	svaf
snared	snaraði
so	á, Sá, svo
soles-of-the-feet	iljarnar
some	nokkur, nokkura
somehow	nokkuð
something	nokkuð
son-of-Asgeir (name)	Ásgeirssonar
son-of-Audun (name)	Auðunarsonar
son-of-Thorkel (name)	Þorkelsson
spoke	mælti
stand	standa
Starkad (name)	Starkaði, Starkaður
stood	Stendur, stóð, stóðu
struck	sló
stubborn	einrænir
such	sjá, slíkum
summer	sumarið
supposed	ætlaði

T, t

terribly	forað, hræðilega, öskurlega
than	en
thanked	þakkaði
that	á, að, er, þá, það, þar
the	á, hið, hinn
the-bed	sæng
the-clock	klukkan
the-clock-sound	klukkuhljóðið
the-demon	Dólgurinn, draugur, draugurinn, púkanum, púki, púkinn, skelmirinn
the-earth	jörðina
the-evening	kveldið
the-flames	eldinum

Word List (English to Old Icelandic)

English	Old Icelandic
the-floor	gólfið
the-Icelander	Íslendingur
the-innermost	innstu
their	sinn
the-kindling	kyndarinn
the-king	konung, konungi, konungs, konungur
the-king's	konungs
them	sér, þeim, þeirra
the-men	menn
then	að, en, þá, þó, því, var
the-night	nátt, náttina
the-outermost	ystu
the-outhouse	heimilishúss
the-oven	ofn
the-place	staðnum
there	þá, þangað, þar
therefore	því
the-serpent	Orminum
the-sound	yminn
the-table	borða
the-torment	fjandunum, píslir
the-worst	verst
they	þér
thick	þykkvan
thin	þunni
this	þess, þetta
this-way	leið
Thorkel (name)	Þorkell
Thorstein (name)	Þorstein, Þorsteini, Þorsteinn
though	þó
thought	þótti, þóttist
three	þrjár
time	tíma
to	að, í, það, til
to-be-helped	hólpinn
together	saman
to-give	gefa
toilet	salerni
told	talað, talaði
to-me	mér
took	tekur, Tók
torment	pína, pínu, písl, píslir
to-the	til
to-us	oss
towards	fram
to-you	þér, yður
travelled	farið
turned	sneri

U, u

English	Old Icelandic
unconscious	óvit
unhurt	klakklaust
un-mighty	ómegin
un-thrown	ósvipt
up	upp
us	vort

V, v

English	Old Icelandic
very-much	mjög
Vik (place)	Víkina

W, w

English	Old Icelandic
warned	varað
war-tooth	hilditönn
was	á, er, var, varð, voru
was-with	var
we	vér
well	vel
went	farið, fór, gekk, gengið, gengu, gengur
were	er, varðst, voru
what	Hvað, Hverja, Hvers
when	En, er
which	er
which-is	sem
while	stund
who	er, Hver, Hverjir, sem
who-was	er
why	Hví
wider	víðara
will	mundu, vil
willed	vildi

Word List (English to Old Icelandic)

English	Old Icelandic
will-you	viltu
winter	veturinn
wish	vil
with	á, með, við
woke-up	vaknaði
wonder	undrast
words	orða
would	mundi, munduð, mundum
wrapped	vafði

Y, y

you	þér, þig, þú
your	yðvar
yours	þér, þitt

A Word Comparison of Old Norse and Old Icelandic Words

Old Norse	Old Icelandic	English
áðr	áður	before
æpði	æpti	shrieked
ætlaða	ætlaði	supposed
aldri	aldrei	never
annat	annað	else
anzaði	ansaði	replied
at	að	about
at	að	as
at	að	at
at	að	from
at	að	that
at	að	then
at	að	to
austr	austur	east
belgði	belgdi	bellowed
betr	betur	better
bezt	best	best
blíðr	blíður	happy
brugðit	brugðið	custom
dólgrinn	dólgurinn	the-demon
draugr	draugur	the-demon
draugrinn	draugurinn	the-demon
ek	eg	I
ek	eg	I-am
ellifu	ellefu	eleven
fætr	fætur	feet
farit	farið	travelled
farit	farið	went
fell	féll	fell
ferr	fer	away
fjölmennr	fjölmennur	followers
fjöndunum	fjandunum	the-torment
foraðs	forað	terribly
gaulat	gaulað	bellow
gengit	gengið	went
gengr	gengur	went
gólfit	gólfið	floor
gólfit	gólfið	the-floor
héðan	héðan	from-here
heldr	heldur	rather
helt	hélt	held
hirðmaðr	hirðmaður	court-man
hræðiliga	hræðilega	terribly
hraustr	hraustur	brave
hváftana	hvoftana	cheeks
hváftunum	hvoftunum	cheeks
hvárum	hvoru	each
hvat	hvað	how
hvat	hvað	what
hvé	hve	how
hverir	hverjir	who
hverr	hver	each
hverr	hver	who
inn	hinn	the
íslendingr	íslendingur	the-Icelander
íslenzkr	íslenskur	Icelandic
it	hið	the
játaði	játtaði	agreed
kemr	kemur	came
klaklaust	klakklaust	unhurt
klukkuhljóðit	klukkuhljóðið	the-clock-sound
kom	komst	came
komit	komið	come
konungr	konungur	the-king
kveldit	kveldið	evening
kveldit	kveldið	the-evening
lengr	lengur	long
liggr	liggur	laid
litit	litið	considered
lítt	líttað	a-little
maðr	maður	a-man
maðr	maður	man
mik	mig	me
mikit	mikið	great
mikit	mikið	much
mjök	mjög	many
mjök	mjög	much
mjök	mjög	very-much
mundið	munduð	would
mundim	mundum	would
niðr	niður	down

A Word Comparison of Old Norse and Old Icelandic

Old Norse	Old Icelandic	English	Old Norse	Old Icelandic	English
nökkura	*nokkura*	some	*varð*	*varðst*	were
nökkurr	*nokkur*	some	*varr*	*var*	aware
nökkut	*nokkuð*	somehow	*várt*	*vort*	us
nökkut	*nokkuð*	something	*váru*	*voru*	was
ok	*og*	and	*váru*	*voru*	were
öklaeld	*ökklaeld*	ankle-fire	*veizlu*	*veislu*	a-feast
Óláfr	*Ólafur*	Olaf (name)	*veizlum*	*veislum*	feasts
Óláfs	*Ólafs*	Olaf's (name)	*verit*	*verið*	been
ópit	*ópið*	open	*vetrinn*	*veturinn*	winter
ópit	*ópið*	shriek	*villtu*	*viltu*	will-you
ór	*úr*	from	*vissa*	*vissi*	knew
ór	*úr*	out-of	*vit*	*við*	knew
öskurliga	*öskurlega*	terribly	*yðr*	*yður*	to-you
Reinu	*Reimi*	Reim (place)	*yrðið*	*yrðuð*	had-been
sængr	*sængur*	bed	*yztu*	*ystu*	the-outermost
sagðr	*sagður*	said			
séð	*séuð*	seem			
setit	*setið*	sat			
sezt	*sest*	sat			
Sigurðr	*Sigurður*	Sigurd (name)			
sik	*sig*	himself			
sjálfr	*sjálfur*	himself			
Starkaðr	*Starkaður*	Starkad (name)			
stendr	*stendur*	stood			
steypðist	*steyptist*	fell			
sumarit	*sumarið*	summer			
sundr	*sundur*	down			
svá	*svo*	so			
talat	*talað*	told			
tekr	*tekur*	took			
þangat	*þangað*	there			
þat	*það*	it			
þat	*það*	that			
þat	*það*	to			
þeira	*þeirra*	them			
þik	*þig*	you			
þokat	*þokað*	moved			
Þorsteirm	*Þorsteinn*	Thorstein (name)			
þóttumst	*þóttist*	thought			
þykkir	*þykir*	seems			
undrumst	*undrast*	wonder			
útan	*utan*	of			
vaknaða	*vaknaði*	woke-up			
varat	*varað*	warned			

www.ingramcontent.com/pod-product-compliance
Lightning Source LLC
Chambersburg PA
CBHW051426070526
44584CB00023B/3604